Contents:

INTRODUCTION

Hello and welcome to this book about "Child Psychology: Prevention of aggressive behaviour".

Nowadays, aggressive behaviour is a common problem that in order to deal with it we must first learn to understand correctly. This is precisely why we have prepared this book in order to provide a detailed and sufficient insight into the nature and characteristics of aggression, its types, the factors that provoke aggressive behaviour, as well as the state, responses and how to recognise the victim of this kind of behaviour.

After all, we have given scientific models that school teachers can best deal with troubled students through concrete actions to minimise aggressive behaviour in the growing generation of children.

What you'll learn?

1. What is aggression.

2. Factors reinforcing the trend of violence.

3. Diagnostic standards of aggression for children.

4. Characteristic features of aggressive children.

5. Conditions and typical reactions of the victim.

6. Signs of recognition of the victim of violence.

7. Brief practical guidance for teachers.

8. Conceptual models to prevent and deal with aggressive and problematic behaviour.

9. Stimulating of a socially acceptable alternative of problematic behaviour.

For whom is this book for:

1. Psychologists

2. Psychiatrist

3. Teachers

4. Pedagogues

5. Social Workers

6. Medical Practitioners

7. Nurses

8. Parents

9. Academician

10. Students

11. Anyone Who Is Interested In: Child Psychology: Prevention of aggressive behaviour.

WHY THIS BOOK AND TOPIC ARE SO IMPORTANT?

In our dynamic everyday life, everyone faces aggression in one form or another. This book is important and useful because we have based it solely on the scientific information we have presented in an easy and accessible way. We have put forward many practical tips on how to deal with aggressive behaviour of others no matter where it comes in your life. We have adhered to the idea of not making the book unnecessarily long, filled with irrelevant and useless information. Everything you find in it can be applied directly to your daily life in one way or another without much effort, cost and time.

ABOUT THE AUTHOR

Valentin Boyadzhiev is a trained nutritionist, graduated Master of Psychology in "Psychology and Psychopathology of Development". He has acquired Professional Qualification "Teacher of Psychology" and Postgraduate Professional Qualification "Psychological Counseling in Psychosomatic and Social Adaptation Disorders". He has obtained a Psychoanalysis Diploma and he is currently specializing in Psychoanalytic Psychotherapy. He is a member of the Association "Bulgarian Psychoanalytic Space", "International Society of Applied Psychoanalysis" and „International Alliance of Holistic Therapists". He is a lecturer on issues related to nutrition,

What you'll learn?

1. What is aggression.

2. Factors reinforcing the trend of violence.

3. Diagnostic standards of aggression for children.

4. Characteristic features of aggressive children.

5. Conditions and typical reactions of the victim.

6. Signs of recognition of the victim of violence.

7. Brief practical guidance for teachers.

8. Conceptual models to prevent and deal with aggressive and problematic behaviour.

9. Stimulating of a socially acceptable alternative of problematic behaviour.

For whom is this book for:

1. Psychologists

2. Psychiatrist

3. Teachers

4. Pedagogues

5. Social Workers

6. Medical Practitioners

7. Nurses

8. Parents

9. Academician

10. Students

11. Anyone Who Is Interested In: Child Psychology: Prevention of aggressive behaviour.

diet, supplementation, food and sports. He is also a teacher and a lecturer in the field of psychology, logic, ethics, law, and philosophy. He has been a school psychologist since 2017. He has been participating annually in scientific conferences on psychology, psychotherapy, dietetics and medicine. His main interest and practice are in the field of psychoanalysis and clinical psychology. For more information about the author, you can check out his official website www.valentinboyadzhiev.com. The working language of the site is Bulgarian, but you can easily translate it.

SPECIAL THANKS

 I would like to express my special thanks to Glory Dimitrova, without whose help this book would not be a fact. She was the person who put a great deal of effort and dedication in the translation of the text and its proper layout. Also, she has a Master Degree in Law and always strives to present our e-books, video certification courses and other activities in the best and most accessible way to a wide audience of interested people.

What is aggression?

The aggression is that kind of behaviour which is oriented to consciously causing different kinds of damage or pain to the people around. It is expressing in the demonstration of hostility or using power against others. The aggression is purposeful, advancing, destructive, violent behaviour which is against contrary to the approved normal standards of behaviour and community rules. It usually leads to psychic stress, low spirits, fear, and pain. The aggression is a common characterization to the kids with behaviour disorders, it is not a model of emotion, motive or routine but a model of manners.

The aggression could be classified into two different sub-specifications: instrumental and impulsive.

1. **Instrumental aggression** - it includes cases when the aggressor attacks other people, but with no bad intention of causing damage or suffer. In concrete, the aggression is used as an instrument for the realization of desired purposes.

2. Impulsive aggression - it includes cases where the concrete goal of the aggressor is consciously causing of damage or suffering to other people.

By the form of acting the aggression could be physical or verbal, active or passive and direct and indirect.

1. Physical aggression - aggressive or criminal deeds whose purpose is to cause harm to people, animals or even to property in rare cases.

2. Verbal aggression - this is a violent behaviour which attempts to cause humiliation, impairment of dignity, abusiveness, a disgrace to a specific person by yelling, threatening, swear-words and other kinds of verbal manifestation.

3. Active aggression - it is represented as kicking, tearing hair, clawing, crushing, pinching, fighting, beating, punching, burning, strangling, poisoning, throwing objects at someone, stabbing, cutting, etc..

4. Direct passive physical aggression - that kind of aggression finds expression in preventing someone from achieving their goals or ignoring the concrete person, neglecting the needs and the desires of someone.

5. Indirect aggression - the damage is inflicted not directly on to the victim itself, but to something owned by the victim or to some other person close to the victim. Per example - this could be causing damages on someone's property like theft or breaking the victim's car or even hurting someone the victim loves.

Various environmental factors could be a good reason to strengthen the tendency of causing violence.

1. Socio-economic crisis and its consequences - that factors threatening the physical survival of particular people and families and it causes spiritual despair and losing faith.

2. Mass media - this one threatens the value system of the young people and it could be said that it provokes the violence usage as an instrument for solving conflicts.

3. Globalization - that factor threatens the self-realization of a person. In a global community, people realize their imperfections and often get into depression.

4. Alienation - this is a threatening factor for the community's cohesion and solidarity, it provokes non-confidence and insecurity.

5. Social devaluation - this is a factor which is threatening the spiritual identity's preservation. The lack of values and orientation of values have a regressive effect on mankind.

The kids obtain knowledge of the behaviour models from three different sources:

1. The first one is the family which can demonstrate aggressive behaviour and at the same time, it could be embedded in the children.

2. From the interaction with their coevals, the children take a first-hand look at the aggression's advantages while playing different games with each other.

3. The children are learning aggressive reactions not only from real-life examples but from symbolic ones. The scenes of violence demonstrated by the movies and the digital games contribute to the increase of aggressive levels in their respective audiences and especially in kids.

Diagnostical standards of aggression for children under school age and young school age

1. The aggressive children often lose control over themselves and even oftener than other kids from their surroundings with a different kind of less aggressive behaviour in comparison to the aggressive ones.

2. The aggressive children argue very often, use profanities, are offensive to other children and even adults.

3. The aggressive children irritate on purpose the adults and decline to obey them, refusing to comply with their requests, advice and rules.

4. The aggressive children often accuse others of something which is part of their own incorrect behaviour and mistakes.

5. They are envious and distrustful.

6. They are also often getting angry and are in conflicts with others.

A child who manifests simultaneously and consistently at least 4 from all the 6 standards from above for a period of six or more months probably have aggression as a quality of its personality and could be called aggressive.

Diagnostical standards of aggression for children in middle school and for the rising generation at school.

1. These aggressive children threaten other people verbally or with gestures, looks, and poses.

2. The initiate physical confrontations.

3. They are using objects which can actually hurt someone in their confrontations.

4. They are physically cruel to people and animals and they are causing pain by all means.

5. The aggressive children could commit theft regarding the people they don't like.

6. They could purposely harm other's property.

7. They are blackmailing people and they are making threats.

8. They are missing from home late at night without their parent's permission.

9. They are also running away from home.

10. They don't go to school at all, they are running from their classes or they are being expelled from school.

A child who manifests a minimum 3 standards of aggression from the above during 6 or more months is considered to have the aggression quality of personality.

Characteristic features of aggressive children

1. They consider a lot of situations as dangerous, threatening and hostile to them.

2. They are oversensitive to a negative attitude towards them.

3. They have the basic adjustment that the others perceive them negatively.

4. They do not estimate their own aggression as aggressive behaviour.

5. They are always accusing their surroundings of something that is part of their own destructive behaviour.

6. In cases of intentional aggression (like assaulting, attacking, destroying someone's property or some other kind of incursion) the aggressive children do not have a sense of guilt or if they do - it is very weakly manifested.

7. They don't take responsibility for their own actions.

8. They have a limited number of reactions in problematical situations.

9. They reveal a low level of empathy in their relationships.

10. They have also a low emotional control.

11. They weakly evaluate their own emotions except for the anger.

12. They are afraid of their parent's unpredictable behaviour.

13. They have neurological disorders; unstable attention; absent-mindedness; weak random access memory of the mind; non-durable memory.

14. They are not able to predict the consequences of their actions (they block their emotions in problematical situations)

15. They have a positive attitude towards the aggression because through the aggressive behaviour they get a feeling of self-significance and personal power.

Special features of aggressive children's families

1. In aggressive children's family, the emotional fondness between the parents and the kids is damaged, especially between the father and the son.

2. Fathers often demonstrate own personal aggressive models of behaviour and also encourage the aggressive behaviour of their little children with an aggressive tendency.

3. The aggressive children's mothers are not demanding and exacting of their kids and often are indifferent to them regarding their social success. The children don't have the exact responsibilities and duties to the family.

4. At the parents of the aggressive children, the models of upbringing and personal behaviour are in conflict with one another and they are being sent mutually exclusive messages and requirements. Usually in that kind of a family are being combined a father with a strong temper and a negligent, thoughtless mother. As a result in the child is formed a model of provocative oppositional behaviour which is transferred to the child's surroundings.

5. The aggressive children's parents often use these main upbringing ways to raise their child:

- physical punishments;

- threats;

- deprivation of privileges;

- introduced restrictions and lack of encouragement;

- often isolation from the other kids;

- consciously depriving of love and care in cases of misdeed.

In these cases, the parents don't have a sense of guilt using that kind of punishments.

6. The aggressive children's parents don't try to understand the reasons for the destructive behaviour of their kids, they are also being indifferent to their emotional life.

Conditions and typical reactions of the victim

The sharpness of the symptomatology depends on different factors like:

- an age;

- a physical and psychical condition of the victim;

- a presence of previous experience with similar situations;

- support from the family, professional and social community;

The sharp stress reaction arise directly at the moment of the stressful event and it is connected to:

- the primary state of numbness;

- narrowing of attention and disorientation;

- the recession from the stressful situation;

- the depression;

- the excessive anxiety, self-isolation;

- an excitement, anger, hyperactivity.

It can be observed partial or complete amnesia about the time of the traumatic event. In similar cases is recommended to help the victim out of the stressful situation quickly. The symptoms usually disappear quickly and then it can be worked painlessly with the victim. If that doesn't happen, the symptoms start to disappear spontaneously after 24-48 hours to three days.

Post-traumatic stress disorder (PTSD) occurs in cases when the traumatic reaction is not well controlled and the victim couldn't deal with the trauma. It is a belated response to the stressful event. The symptoms of post-traumatic stress disorder are:

- episodes of repeated experience of the trauma such as suddenly remembering of particular fragments of the situation;

- experiences in the form of dreams, nightmares;

- continuing sense of numbness and emotional dullness;

- a manifestation of hostility to others;

- loss of appetite, mood, sleep disorders;

- avoidance of activities and signals resembling the traumatic situation;

Reactions in the victim other than traumatic and post-traumatic stress

- Guilt and self-accusation. This symptomatology is spread in sexual offenses and domestic violence. This feeling is often inculcated by the abuser to ensure silence from the victim.

- A sense of helplessness and fear. The generating of fear and anxiety as an effect of violence could lead to negative changes in the social behaviour of the victim and this way it compromises the sense of protection of the abused one.

- Paradoxical situations such as laughter or devaluation of what happened.

- Uncontrollable anger, aggression and redirecting the furious reactions towards a neutral subject, mostly towards the representatives of the law. This is a common situation which is paradoxical in domestic violence. The victim feels the need of immediate emotional relief because anger is an intense emotional state. The oppressor is the object of anger but the relations between victim and oppressor do not always allow adequate relief of the emotions and in which case anger is being redirected towards a more accessible object.

What is the experience of victims of violence?

The systemic and incidental experience of violence can lead to changes of the personality. A person who is mistreated, humiliated, hurt or raped lives in fear. The fear changes the self-confidence of the victim. The fear provokes:

- low self-esteem and devaluation of life;

- hatred of oneself;

- compliance with the abuser's requirements;

- denial of one's own opinion;

- compromise with own principles and needs;

- a sense of guilt and helplessness;

- abuse of various substances;

- chronic anxiety;

- membership in various groups;

The victim is frustrated by the interpersonal interaction and the perspective of life loses meaning. A life 'without a compass' is a precondition for self-isolation and a prerequisite for aggression or self-aggression.

Signs for recognizing a victim of violence

Children - closeness (apathy), aggressive behaviour, a weeping cry, emotional dependence, avoiding eye contact, indiscriminating affection. In the case of sexual violence - sexual behaviour, rigidity, emotional dependence, passiveness, closeness, overexcitement, difficulty feeding.

Adolescent - closeness (apathy), aggressive and self-destructive behaviour, self-harming, problems at school, fear of failure, abuse of various substances, escape from home. In the case of sexual violence - sexual behaviour, inability to attach to coevals, distraction, feeding disorders (bulimia, anorexia, obesity), problems in school.

Young Adult - closeness (apathy), aggressive and anti-social behaviour, failure to understand coevals and seeking the attention of the adults, escape from home and use of alcohol, narcotics, and other substances, problems at school. In the case of sexual violence - sexual behaviour, posturing, debauchery and prostitution, disobedience or irreconcilability, that is being brought to extreme isolation, fear, self-harm, suicidal symptoms, pseudo-maturity, eating disorders, abuse of alcohol or narcotics, escape from home.

Adults - inability to maintain long and satisfying relationships, low self-esteem, a manifestation of fear, anger, and situations of violence. In the case of sexual violence - sexual problems, mistrust, body shame, inability of self-assertion, victimisation, alcohol or drug abuse, low self-esteem.

Brief practical guidance for teachers

1. Reducing access to the victims - When the students who show aggression are grouped together for an education in the classroom, then it is very possible that there may be sworn enemies among the group as well as potential victims of the more dominant youths. Sometimes the mere presence of a potential victim is an event that is triggered. Access to the victims can be reduced by placement or grouping, which ensures that the aggressor and the potential victim are separated.

2. Setting reasonable norms and expectations - The class needs functional and realistic expectations that the students have the skills to achieve. If the rules and the expectations are appropriate and realistic, then most of the students have a chance to achieve them.

3. Avoid confrontation - It is important for the teachers to avoid confrontation with aggressive youths when it is possible. The teacher may later talk to the student instead of publicly reprimanding him.

4. Reducing competition - The competition in the classroom can be minimized in several ways. Each child can only be compared for assessment purposes.

5. Using non-verbal signals and reminders - Oral verdicts have been found to reinforce provocative behaviour. Pupils who have a tendency to aggressive behaviour seem to respond well to the use of signals rather than to the teacher's slanging.

6. Ensuring constant supervision - 'The Golden Rule' for teachers of students with aggressive and violent behaviour is 'never leave them alone and never turn your back' (Guetzloe, 1991).

7. Warning signs of a violent episode - The identification of signs, signals or other incentives that usually precede a violent episode can help prevent the crisis. if we leave today's problem unresponsive, tomorrow it may deepen and turn into aggression and violence

8. Reaction to a student who loses control - The steps you need to follow during an aggressive or violent episode must be rehearsed until they become automatic so that when the student shows signs of impending loss of control, the plan can be followed without hesitation.

The human brain works automatically and quickly with an emotional stimulus, generating unconscious responses (Bargh and Morsella 2008).

Concrete actions:

- Play the role of calm and cool. Action in this way actually helps one to stay calm.

- Be direct, but not aggressive. Do not threaten the student verbally or physically.

- Force the student into a conversation, so you can handle the situation easier with him/her.

Conceptual models to prevent and deal with aggressive and problematic behaviour

Ignoring - Often, some problematic behaviour is demonstrated in order to attract and retain the attention of the teacher for a longer time. When this is certainly established, the best behavioural therapy technique would be ignoring the student's behaviour, which means that the teacher should ignore the student's poor behaviour and thus does not encourage him to re-apply it. For example, when a student wants to keep his attention on himself, he screams, calls and throws objects around, rolls, kicks children, kicks them. If a teacher approaches and spends a dozen minutes trying to calm the student and explain that such behaviour is bad, then the student will actually achieve his goal by drawing the attention of the teacher and forcing him to devote more time to himself/herself. If the teacher completely ignores the behaviour of the student who shouts and throws objects and takes the other children around him by dealing only with them, then the aggressive student will not be able to draw the attention of the teacher with such behaviour and may stop applying the aggressive model more or less so often. However, when the reason for the unacceptable behaviour is not to attract attention, then the ignoring can be extremely dangerous, as it will encourage the aggressive behaviour of the student through his untimely correction. That's why the functional evaluation should be done very carefully and competently before ignoring it as a method of coping with problem behaviour.

Verbal punishments - This method does not allow the teacher to lose his nerves and to raise a scandal of the scholar and to call him offensive names but gives a brief and clear verbal disapproval of the student's behaviour. Here are some guidelines for making good use of verbal punishments:

- Be clear and tell the student what you do not approve of in his behaviour.

- Verbal punishment should be done immediately after demonstrating problem behaviour.

- Do not scream at the student, the slight decrease in the usual voice is enough.

- If necessary, back the verbal penalty with deprivation of privileges.

- Encourage your student to behave well by including instructions on what behaviour you would approve in the verbal punishment.

- Be as relaxed as possible and do not lose control of yourself.

- After performing a verbal punishment, do not remind the student about the demonstrative problem behaviour.

- Observe the student's response to verbal punishment and consider whether this method has an effect.

Deprivation of privileges - Deprivation of privileges is a negative promotion, which may eventually lead to positive results. It is desirable that the deprivation of privileges has a logical connection with the demonstrated problem behaviour and to be a direct consequence of it. For example, if a student refuses to participate in activities during a class, he/she may be deprived of free time during breaks. Here are some guidelines that can be followed when the teacher applies the method of deprivation of privileges:

- Ensure that the student understands the connection between the problematic behaviour and the deprivation of privileges.

- Be fair in deprivation of privileges.

- Do not discuss with the student the question of depriving him of privileges once you have imposed them.

- Do not feel guilty about the fact that you have deprived the student of privileges. Every student is familiar with the rules of conduct and everybody knows that their violation leads to certain consequences.

Timeout - Timeout is a sports term that can also be applied in behavioural therapy. In general, this means that when a student demonstrates problematic behaviour, it is because of his shift from the usual environment - for example, another place in the classroom or another classroom. Often, the classrooms of students with multiple disabilities provide a space for relaxation that is separated by something like a screen or a cupboard from the common room. This is a good place where the student can be left alone for some time after having demonstrated a problem behaviour. In cases where the student is raging and when there is a risk of injuring himself or others or causing material damage, then he can be taken to another room where he is not a danger to anyone. The duration of timeout has to be carefully calculated - it should not be too short so that the student could not understand the purpose of it, it also shouldn't be long enough to cause emotional problems for the student, or it should not be misinterpreted as a reward or giving a break. The timeout duration depends on the depth of manifestation and the duration of aggressive behaviour. Usually, two to five minutes are sufficient for this method of behavioural therapy, unless there are some other conditions and causes.

Oversaturation - The oversaturation is a method of eliminating the undesired behaviour through its overprotection, exaggeration and over-stimulation. Often, people tend to oversaturate themselves of different things and cease to consider them pleasant and interesting and they voluntarily give them up. This also applies to the problematic behaviour - its over-stimulation and enhancement will gradually lead to a loss of interest in demonstrating it. For example, if the student has the habit of taking teaching and other materials from his classmates without their permission and consent, the teacher can apply the method of oversaturation. He can collect all pencils, crayons, and other materials in the classroom and place them on a desk in front of the student, while at the same time engaging other students in other activities, such as reading a fairy tale, puppet theatre, or anything else. This should be repeated day by day until the student loses interest in owning all the materials in the classroom, given to him voluntarily, and at the same time, the others are busy with other interesting activities.

Penalties / Sanctions - The penalties/sanctions are as old and well-known, as well as poorly understood and often misinterpreted method of behavioural therapy. They should be used only as a method of procedure designed to reduce or eliminate the inappropriate behaviour and not as a way for the student to be made to suffer for a particular behaviour. Often, punishments are intertwined and partially overlap with others, discussed previously, methods of behavioural therapy such as deprivation of privileges and unpleasant consequences. The penalties should exclude any form of physical use of force such as hitting or injuring the student. They can by no means involve the deprivation of the disciple from food, use of a toilet or sleep. Penalties should be well-chosen and considered and fairly imposed. It is important for the student to understand the punishment as a consequence of their own inappropriate behaviour and to link the demonstration of such behaviour with the imposition of a penalty in the future.

Stimulating of a socially acceptable alternative of problematic behaviour.

Positive stimulation - Positive stimulation can be material, social or personal.

- Social encouragement – praise, approval, hair stroking, shoulder tap.

- Material encouragement (a.k.a. real or psychological encouragement) – food, candy or any other material prise. In this category are also different types of psychological encouragement, like the use of a special symbol (seal) in the notebook or worksheet as a sign of approval, marking with a red dot.

- Personal encouragement – this is the stimulation of the internal feeling of self-satisfaction from the completion of a task or a well-done job. This type of encouragement usually is used to stimulate a deeper feeling of pride.

Figuration - The method of figuration is similar to the task of a sculptor, shaping his sculpture. In the case of behaviour therapy, this means that it is the teacher's responsibility to form the want in the student to exhibit a proper, socially acceptable behaviour. The way that the affirmation of such a positive behaviour is achieved by the teacher by the use of positive reinforcement whenever the student exhibits it. It is a requirement to have a systematic positive reinforcement every time after the student exhibits such behaviour.

Negotiation - The method of negotiation is extremely popular, and most teachers and parents utilize it while dealing with their students or children even without realizing it. Negotiation is each verbal or written contract between two or more individuals or groups, in which the sides participating in it agree to undertake specific obligations for which they receive certain benefits. Here are some examples of daily occurrence of negotiations: "After you finish this, you can listen to music.", "Eat your food and after we will go out.", "If you behave in the next 15 minutes you are going to get a biscuit." Negotiation as a method of Behaviour therapy needs to follow specific rules:

- It must be systematic and precise.

- It must provide benefits that are appropriate for the student – for example, if the student is overweight food should not be used as a reward too often in the negotiation process.

- After the negotiation is complete, both sides need to fulfil the obligations they have agreed to – example, if the student fulfils the task that was set to him, the teacher needs to provide him with the agreed compensation or benefit.

Reward - Receiving a reward for a job well done or for demonstrating good behaviour is a common practise in schools. The reward is every encouragement of the desired behaviour. This encouragement also needs to be significant and important to the student. Sometimes the teacher offers as a reward activities or items that have no value to the students, thus failing to encourage him to fulfil the task at hand or exhibit the desired behaviour. Thus, rewards should be valued and picked carefully. In the table below you can see some examples of appropriate rewards, which can be used as stimulation of good behaviour and their continuation.

Sampling - Human behaviour is best taught through the use of observation and imitation. As a method in behaviour therapy sampling means the imitation of specific behaviour (if it is appropriate) or not to be imitated (it's inappropriate) from the student. This is one of the oldest and most commonly used methods of behaviour therapy. Often teachers and parents apply it unconsciously by saying something in the lines of: "Be goods and obedient like your sister.", "Can you also write beautifully and legibly as Annie?" or "Why can't you be good behaved like all the other boys and girls at your age?". For the success of this method, it is a requirement to pick examples with people that are important and respected by the student that he also like or loves – favourite classmate, favourite teacher or member of the team, favourite artist, singer, and others. We also need to select a specific behaviour in the person that we are using for the sampling instead of trying to force the student to imitate every aspect of the behaviour of set personality – something that would be hard for a student with a lot if psychological disabilities to begin with. For example, we can use a favourite classmate as a behaviour model for keeping quiet while eating lunch or a favourite teacher as a model for a clean and well-dressed person.